BECOMING A
CITIZEN

ADOPTING A NEW HOME

Fred Bratman

A Blackbirch Graphics Book

RSVP

RAINTREE
STECK-VAUGHN
P U B L I S H E R S

Austin, Texas

A Blackbirch Graphics Book

Printed and bound in Mexico

1 2 3 4 5 6 7 8 9 0   RRD   98 97 96 95 94 93

Library of Congress Cataloging-in-Publication Data

Bratman, Fred.
    Becoming a citizen: adopting a new home / Fred Bratman
      p.   cm. — (Good citizenship library)
    Includes bibliographical references (p.) and index.
    Summary: Discusses the law, the court system, how the law can be challenged, and what our laws mean to the individual.
    ISBN 0-8114-7354-6 — ISBN 0-8114-5582-3 (softcover)
    1. United States—Emigration and immigration—History—Juvenile literature. 2. Citizenship—United States—Juvenile literature. I. Title. II. Series.
JV6450.B74 1993
323.6'0973—dc20

          92-24061
          CIP
          AC

Acknowledgments and Photo Credits

Cover: ©Greenwood/Gamma-Liaison; p. 4: ©Daemmrich; p. 6: AP/Wide World Photos; pp. 8, 9, 12, 17: North Wind Picture Archives; p. 11: ©David Valdez/The White House; pp. 18, 20: Culver Pictures; p. 21: National Portrait Gallery, Smithsonian Institute; p. 22: AP/Wide World Photos; p. 27: ©Michael J. Howell; p. 29: ©Bruce Glassman; p. 31: ©Judy Sloan/Gamma-Liaison; p. 32: Wide World Photos; p. 35: ©P. Chartrand/Gamma-Liaison; p. 39: ©Carol Halebian/Gamma-Liaison; p. 41: Liaison Agency; p. 42: ©Daniel Simon/Gamma-Liaison; p. 45: ©Ogust/The Image Works.

Photo research by Grace How

Contents

Citizenship

Most people born in the United States take their citizenship for granted. They were born with it. They didn't voyage across deadly oceans in unseaworthy ships, or face long years of waiting for a prized visa to the United States. Most Americans don't give a second thought to the rights and privileges that they enjoy as U.S. citizens. These rights, which the U.S. Constitution spells out, range from freedom of speech to freedom of religion to the right to a fair and speedy trial.

But millions of people all around the world dream of becoming U.S. citizens. When they compare the United States to their own nations, they see this country as a land of vast economic

Opposite:
America's citizens come from many different cultures and ethnic groups.

5

opportunity and a place where citizens play an active role in shaping and even deciding a government's direction.

Other Nations, Other Rights

Many other nations deny citizens these basic rights. Often, citizenship is open to only a few people, and even then few rights are granted. For many years in South Africa, for instance, the whites, who control the government, treated blacks as second-class citizens. Blacks were not allowed to hold certain jobs and could not play a full role in the political system. This racial policy is called "apartheid." Only recently has the South African government taken action to abolish apartheid. In

Citizens in some countries are denied rights that many Americans take for granted. In South Africa, the government enforced segregation and racism for hundreds of years.

March 1992 the citizens of South Africa voted to gradually rid their country of this racially biased political system.

In China and Cuba, the state authorities deny the average citizen any say in government policy. Those who speak out against the system are often in danger of arrest and imprisonment. These governments have denied fair trials to people they accused of wrongdoing, and have even executed them.

Despite the many hardships they may face, millions of people yearn to come to the United States. They want to enjoy the freedoms that are available to U.S. citizens—freedoms greater than the few available in these "less free nations."

Like almost every nation, the United States has an immigration policy that determines how many people can come into the country. Historically, the policy has been tied to the country's need for workers: As more workers were needed, the number of foreigners allowed to come in rose. The number dropped and restrictions were tightened when the United States faced tougher economic times and a high rate of unemployment.

In the simplest terms, citizenship is a partnership between an individual and the state. It is a contract that guarantees certain rights to the individual but also imposes many responsibilities. There is also an understanding that both sides will live up to their ends of the bargain. When one side falls short, the partnership is threatened.

Citizens of ancient Greece were required to vote, serve on juries, and serve in the military. They were also required to pay taxes for the running of their government.

Countries differ in their views of this balance. In a democracy—the form of government under which the United States operates—the government is believed to get its power from the people. In a dictatorship, the government—which is usually one person or a small group of people—is believed to be the supreme source of all the power and rights. A dictatorship can give or not give power to the people as it chooses.

The Origins of Citizenship

Most historians agree that true citizenship first developed in ancient Greece about 2,500 years ago and then later in Rome. The rights of citizens in these societies were very limited. Citizens were allowed to own land and they played some role in government. However, these rights were primarily limited to men who owned property. What's more, slavery was permitted, and slaves had no rights.

With Greek citizens' rights also came responsibilities. Citizens were required to vote, sit on juries, and serve in the military.

The history of citizenship has seen many steps forward as well as backward. For more than 1,000 years, especially during the 1500s and 1600s, kings and queens ruled many countries. Such rulers are called monarchs. Some of these monarchs gave the people they ruled some rights, but many kings and queens were harsh and cruel, badly treating their subjects, the people they ruled. A monarch could make a decision without consulting anyone else, if he or she so chose.

The nature of citizenship changed drastically during the 1700s, when democracies sprouted up following the American and French revolutions. After these successful rebellions, the absolute rule of monarchs was eliminated in these countries. Subjects became citizens, no longer pledging their loyalty to an individual or sovereign but to the entire nation.

During the 1500s and 1600s, many countries were ruled by strict monarchs who granted few rights to people they ruled. King Henry VIII was one of England's harshest and most unyielding kings.

9

Citizenship in the United States

In the United States, the Constitution guarantees equal protection of the law to all citizens. The color, race, or religion of the individual is not allowed to matter. In reality, of course, it sometimes does.

In a democracy, citizens can play a big role in shaping the decisions a country makes. The desires and opinions of citizens can influence elected lawmakers. Since citizens have the right to vote, they can elect officials whose political ideas they share. If they are unhappy with an elected official, they can vote for someone else in the next election. Citizens even have the right to run for political office themselves.

People born in the United States don't have to face the ordeal that foreigners face in order to become a citizen. Birth in the United States automatically assures the individual U.S. citizenship. U.S.-born people are called native citizens.

Foreigners, or aliens, can become naturalized citizens if they fulfill certain requirements. Naturalized citizens are entitled to the same rights that native citizens enjoy with one exception. A naturalized citizen cannot become president or vice-president of the United States. The nation's top two offices are open only to native-born citizens. This law aims at assuring that the president's loyalty and allegiance is to this nation.

The residents of several islands that are under U.S. control enjoy some of the rights of U.S.

citizens but not all. These islands include Puerto Rico, the Virgin Islands, Guam, and American Samoa. In addition, residents of Washington, D.C., have all rights of citizens but can't vote for president. And their delegate to Congress doesn't have a vote.

U.S. citizens who abuse any of their rights and privileges can find themselves facing the possibility of losing their citizenship. This is an extremely rare occurrence in recent times. Still, U.S. citizens who serve in the armed forces of a foreign nation may be stripped of their U.S. citizenship.

The offices of president and vice-president of the United States are open only to native-born citizens. President George Bush served in both offices during his political career.

11

★ ★ ★ ★ THE SLAVE TRADE: A SAD CHAPTER IN ★ ★ ★ ★
U.S. HISTORY

Unlike any other ethnic or racial group, almost all African Americans were brought to this country against their will as slaves. For over 100 years they were denied the most basic of human rights, and considered the property of their owners.

The slave trade began in the mid-1600s, while this country was still a colony of England. Slavery existed in many other parts of the world. Slaves were primarily brought here to work on large farms, or plantations, in Southern communities. They worked in the fields picking cotton and harvesting tobacco.

The plantations needed large numbers of laborers to cultivate these crops. The slaves who didn't work in the fields, where they were known as field hands, worked as servants in their owners' homes. They were called house slaves.

Slaves helped the nation's economy grow. They made cotton the country's largest crop for export. Slaves also helped build railroads and roads.

In the Northern colonies few people owned slaves. They had less economic need for them. In the North, farms were smaller and needed less help. In addition, the North's economy focused on industry. Factories required more skilled workers than slaves.

The drive to end slavery in the United States, called the abolitionist movement, started in the 1800s. The abolitionists considered slavery immoral. They argued that all people were created equal. But those who supported slavery said slavery was a law of nature, and it was only right that the strong should rule the weak.

For most slaves life was hard. Field hands worked from sunrise to sunset. Most slaves lived in horrible conditions. Often more than a dozen people were squeezed into each room of the slave shacks.

Viewed as the property of their owners, slaves did not have individual rights. They could not marry, own property, or even work for their own freedom like indentured servants. What was worse, families of slaves were often broken up on the auction block, with mothers sold separately from their children.

In 1808, Congress outlawed the importation of African slaves into the United States. Even so, the number of slaves kept growing, as slaves already in the United States were encouraged to reproduce. By 1860, one year before the Civil War, the number of slaves in the South had grown to one million, nearly three times the number when Congress had banned further importation in 1808.

In 1857, a slave from Missouri asked the U.S. Supreme Court for his freedom. Dred Scott argued that because he had lived with his owner for three years in Illinois and in the Wisconsin Territory (two areas that prohibited slavery), he was a freeman. A lower court ruled that Scott was right, but the Supreme Court disagreed. The nation's highest court ruled that blacks were not U.S. citizens and not entitled even to bring their complaints to court. Dred Scott's story had a happier ending. Shortly after the court's ruling, he was sold to a new owner who set Scott free.

The Civil War (1861-1865) ended slavery in the United States and reversed the court's decision. The Thirteenth Amendment to the U.S. Constitution made African Americans citizens, and the Fourteenth Amendment gave them the right to vote.

Similarly, for much of U.S. history Native Americans were denied rights enjoyed by other citizens. For most of the 1800s, the federal government viewed Indians as dangerous savages. After decades of wars and tens of thousands of deaths, Native Americans were settled (often by force) on reservations, where they were given some self-rule. About two million Native Americans now live in the United States, about half of them on reservations.

A slave auction in the 1800s.

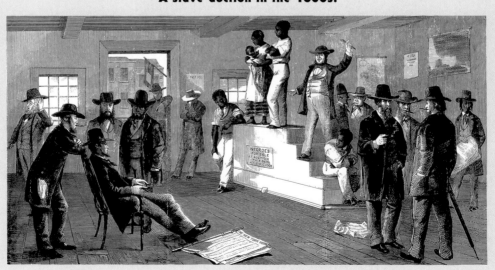

Most immigrants from America's second wave were Irish or German. Here, Irish immigrants gather just before docking in New York.

The Irish, who were escaping a deadly potato famine, came with little money, while the Germans arrived with some savings. The Irish usually stayed where they arrived, mostly in Eastern cities such as Philadelphia and New York. The Germans had enough money to travel by train to the Midwest. Many went to Chicago and from there established farms in areas as far west as Colorado.

By the mid-1850s, New York had replaced Philadelphia as the nation's chief port for welcoming immigrants. In 1855, the United States' first station for processing immigrants opened in what had been Castle Garden, at the southern tip of Manhattan, in New York. Ellis Island, the most famous of such stations, opened in 1892.

As America grew, the need for workers rose. Employers hired agents in Europe to recruit people to come to the United States. Workers were needed to build the railroads that were expanding westward and to work in the coal mines. The work was hard, dangerous, and poorly paid.

Immigrants were often crammed on dirty and unseaworthy vessels for the voyage to the United States. Some ships never made it, and many lives were lost at sea. For instance, the crossing from England to the United States was advertised to take six weeks, but often took twice as long. The trip became easier after steam-powered engines replaced sails on large ships. By 1900, the number of deaths at sea dropped steeply.

By the mid-1800s, immigration to California rose sharply. News of the discovery of gold lured people from the eastern U.S. to travel across the continent. Immigrants from China traveled across the Pacific. But the Chinese immigrants were not welcomed. Native-born Americans and European immigrants resented them. They accused the Chinese of working for extremely low wages, making it hard for others to find jobs. Mobs even attacked the Chinese immigrants. In the late 1870s, many Californians demanded laws to keep out Chinese immigrants. Because the United States had a treaty with China, the government at first resisted. But in 1882, political pressures caused the Congress to pass the Chinese Exclusion Act, which restricted Chinese immigration for the next 10 years.

The Know-Nothing Party

As the number of immigrants grew, Americans began to fear the newcomers. They said the newcomers were taking jobs from many native-born Americans. They feared that they stood to lose out if more people were allowed into the United States. Those who opposed these immigrants banded together to form the American party, also known as the Know-Nothing party. The party resented the surge of Irish and German immigrants. Many of these immigrants lived in urban areas controlled by corrupt politicians. Many of them were also Roman Catholics, and many Protestants at that time thought Catholics weren't Christians. They believed that the Catholic church was the work of the devil, and that people who belonged to it couldn't be trusted.

The Know-Nothing party got its unusual nickname from an often repeated phrase. When a member was asked about what the party stood for, he or she would say, "I know nothing." The Know-

The Know-Nothing party was organized as a reaction against the wave of immigration that took place in the 1800s.

Millard Fillmore ran for president as the Know-Nothing party's candidate in 1856.

Nothing party called for a dramatic increase in the number of years it took to become a citizen. The party also wanted to ban foreign-born citizens from holding political office.

The party's popularity peaked in 1856, when its presidential candidate, Millard Fillmore, captured 21 percent of the vote. Afterward, the party faded away. Many Americans, however, continued to resent foreigners.

In 1875, the United States imposed laws for the first time that limited who could immigrate here. Convicts and prostitutes, who made up a sizable number of early newcomers, were now barred.

Later Immigration

 By 1870, the United States was in the midst of an economic depression. Immigration again slowed. But in 1881 the third and most dramatic jump in immigration began. During the next 40 years more than 23 million immigrants landed in America.

This third wave of immigrants was different from the two earlier ones. Up until then, the immigrants had come primarily from northern and western Europe. But during the third wave most of the immigrants came from southern and eastern Europe, with some others from Asia.

For these new immigrants, which is what they were called to distinguish them from the earlier immigrants, starting life in the United States was

Opposite:
An Italian family arrives on Ellis Island in 1905.

23

extremely difficult. Few knew the language or customs, and many were penniless. After passing through Ellis Island, many of the immigrants were left to fend for themselves. There were virtually no government programs to help immigrants adjust to their new home. Some unscrupulous individuals took advantage of these newcomers, conning them out of the few dollars or possessions that they had brought with them.

Living conditions were harsh. Immigrants rented rooms that were dirty firetraps. Finding work was hard, and the pay was meager. Often, a family earned extra money by sitting around the kitchen table for 16 hours a day stitching garments. The light in these crowded tenements was dim and the air was rank and stale.

Despite these hardships, immigrants kept on coming. They refused to give up their dream. They saw the United States as a place where they could get a new start no matter what their origin.

Some people welcomed the idea of people from many lands coming to America. They viewed the country as a "melting pot," where all these different races would be transformed into a new people—the Americans. But others were frightened, and as the number of new immigrants grew, so did hatred toward them. Many native-born Americans believed that the unity of the country was in grave danger of crumbling. They argued that the new immigrants—especially Asians—didn't share the same customs and values. The resentment turned to anger and sometimes led to violence. Jews, Roman Catholics, and Japanese were attacked.

In 1882, with tempers heating up, Congress enacted a law that prohibited Chinese immigrants from coming to the United States. The government also widened the categories of people banned to include beggars and unaccompanied minors. The number of such laws increased. Immigrants were required to know how to read and write, and in 1917 another law barred most Asians from entering.

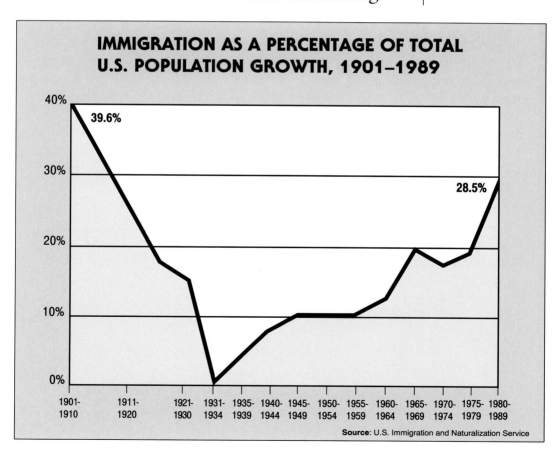

IMMIGRATION AS A PERCENTAGE OF TOTAL U.S. POPULATION GROWTH, 1901–1989

39.6%

28.5%

| 1901-1910 | 1911-1920 | 1921-1930 | 1931-1934 | 1935-1939 | 1940-1944 | 1945-1949 | 1950-1954 | 1955-1959 | 1960-1964 | 1965-1969 | 1970-1974 | 1975-1979 | 1980-1989 |

Source: U.S. Immigration and Naturalization Service

THE STATUE OF LIBERTY: A SHINING TORCH OF FREEDOM

For millions of immigrants arriving in the United States, the Statue of Liberty was the first sight of the New World. To these immigrants, the statue held the promise of a new and better life. The huge statue towers above Liberty Island and has become a symbol of freedom to people everywhere.

It took more than 20 years from the time when the idea for such a monument was broached until its official dedication on October 28, 1886. At times, it didn't look as if the statue would be completed, as money for its construction ran perilously low.

The statue was a gift of the people of France to the United States. Frédéric August Bartholdi, a French sculptor, designed the statue and chose Liberty Island, which is near Ellis Island, as its home. The idea for the statue didn't come from Bartholdi but from a French historian, Édouard-René Lefebvre de Laboulaye.

But it took ten years before the construction of the statue of a robed woman holding a torch actually began in France. Construction was a big and difficult task. Bartholdi first made a clay figure of what he had in mind. Then three plaster models followed. Each was larger than the one before it. Later, wooden forms were constructed, and metal sheets were bent into shape.

Still, there was the engineering problem of keeping such a large statue standing. Alexandre Gustave Eiffel, a French engineer and the builder of Paris's Eiffel Tower, designed a support system. He connected the statue's copper skin to an iron tower with iron bars.

On July 4, 1884, Bartholdi presented the statue to the United States. The construction of the pedestal, however, had yet to be completed. Richard Morris Hunt, a U.S. architect, was designing the pedestal, but money ran out. A New York newspaper launched a campaign to raise the funds, and within weeks it raised enough to complete the pedestal.

The statue, from its feet to the top of the torch, is 151 feet and 1 inch high. It weighs 225 tons. The copper skin is only 3/32 of an inch thick. Inside, two parallel staircases climb up to the crown, which also includes an observation deck.

While one hand holds a torch, the other one cradles a tablet with the date of the Declaration of Independence. A broken chain lies at the statue's feet.

In 1903, a poem by Emma Lazarus was placed on the statues's pedestal. Here is part of the poem:

". . . Give me your tired, your poor,

Your huddled masses yearning to breathe free,

The wretched refuse of your teeming shore.

Send these, the homeless, tempest-tost, to me,

I lift my lamp beside the golden door!"

The statue attracts more than two million visitors a year.

As Congress enacted these laws the number of immigrants diminished. By 1921, the third wave ended as Congress put a limit on the number of people allowed to enter. Congress created a quota system that said that the number of immigrants from a country would be based on the number of the foreign-born people of that nationality who already lived here.

From the 1920s until 1965, immigration fell. People not only did not come in such large numbers; some even left. The Depression of the 1930s, which quickly led to high unemployment, encouraged people to leave. Almost all economic opportunities dried up. During World War II, after the United States and China became allies, the federal government lifted the ban on Chinese immigration. After the war, the United States admitted 600,000 Europeans who had been left homeless. These people were called refugees. They had nowhere else to go. In 1952, the law restricting other Asian immigration was reversed.

The Fourth Wave

The fourth wave began in 1965, when the quota system was drastically altered. The quota was no longer based on nationality, but on hemisphere. The government set an annual ceiling of 170,000 immigrants from the Eastern Hemisphere and 120,000 from the Western Hemisphere. As a result, the percentage of immigrants from Europe

During the 1980s, Asians from the Philippines, China, South Korea, and Vietnam have dominated American immigration. Here, a Korean grocer sells his produce in an open-air market.

dropped, while that from Asia and the West Indies jumped. In 1980 the allocation of hemispheres was dropped, and a worldwide annual total of 270,000 was set.

Today the largest number of legal immigrants come from Mexico, the Philippines, Haiti, South Korea, and China. What's more, the East Coast is no longer the favorite spot for newcomers to settle in. California and Florida attract the majority of these latest immigrants.

Besides legal immigrants, hundreds of thousands of people sneak into the United States. These

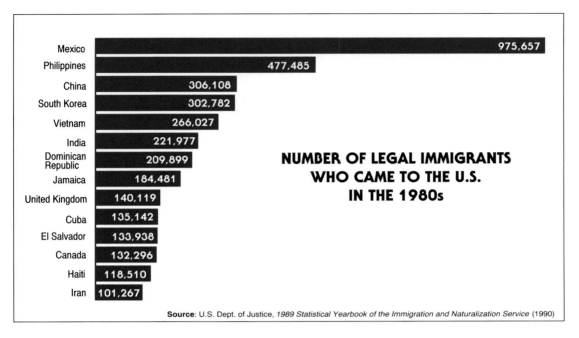

Mexico	975,657
Philippines	477,485
China	306,108
South Korea	302,782
Vietnam	266,027
India	221,977
Dominican Republic	209,899
Jamaica	184,481
United Kingdom	140,119
Cuba	135,142
El Salvador	133,938
Canada	132,296
Haiti	118,510
Iran	101,267

NUMBER OF LEGAL IMMIGRANTS WHO CAME TO THE U.S. IN THE 1980s

Source: U.S. Dept. of Justice, *1989 Statistical Yearbook of the Immigration and Naturalization Service* (1990)

people come because they are often desperate to escape the poverty of their own homelands. Unlike legal immigrants, illegal aliens often come here as students or visitors but don't leave when their visa, or permission to stay, expires. Others sneak across the border. There are as many as five million illegal aliens in the United States.

In 1986, the federal government established an amnesty program for illegal aliens who had lived or worked in the United States for a set period of time. Illegal aliens were told to apply for a pardon. By the end of the program, nearly two years later, more than three million aliens had asked for amnesty. But many thousands had not. They complained that the government forms confused them and many didn't have the records needed to prove that they had lived here.

Soviet Immigration

In the late 1980s, immigration from the former Soviet Union surged. For decades Soviet citizens had found it next to impossible to leave. This was especially true for Jews. The state authorities placed heavy restrictions on those wishing to emigrate.

But these restrictions were eased a great deal as the Communist government's power collapsed. Although many of the Jewish émigrés went to Israel, thousands came to the United States. Many settled in Brighton Beach, Brooklyn, which won the nickname Odessa-by-the-Sea.

Most of the new immigrants have embraced the customs and values of the United States. They live productive lives, contributing to the strength of the nation. As many of the new immigrants are better educated than earlier ones, they have made great contributions in science, medicine, and computer technology.

Two Russian émigrés walk along the boardwalk in Brighton Beach, New York.

4

Becoming a U.S. Citizen

Becoming a U.S. citizen is not an easy task. It requires patience, perseverance, and a dose of good luck. If nothing else, the paperwork alone often can be quite overwhelming.

The first step on the long road to becoming a U.S. citizen is for a foreigner to get to the United States. This alone usually requires some doing. The trip alone can be costly.

The Temporary Visa

But even before a foreigner boards a plane or ship, he must obtain permission from the United States. Such permission is called a visa. There are two basic kinds of visas available. The easiest one to obtain is a

Opposite:
Five aliens from the Boston area proudly display cards that grant them amnesty and allow them to be eligible for permanent residency in America.

33

temporary visa, which is what tourists get to visit the United States. A temporary visa has a time limit on it, usually of six months. Sometimes, foreigners will come to the United States on a temporary visa and then seek an "adjustment of status" that allows them to stay permanently.

Although getting a temporary visa as a tourist is usually easy, the Immigration and Naturalization Service (INS), an agency of the U.S. Department of Justice, can deny the request. It has the authority to do so under the McCarran-Walter Act of 1952. This act says that the country can refuse to let in people who have contagious diseases or other medical or mental problems. It also says the INS can reject those who the agency believed might try to overthrow the government.

Sometimes people are stopped right at the border. Authors such as Carlos Fuentes and Gabriel García Márquez have been denied entry because of their political views.

Immigrant Visas

The INS also issues immigrant visas, which are the type of visa that is most prized by those wishing to live in the United States permanently. In most cases, a foreigner applies for an immigrant visa at the U.S. embassy or consulate in his or her homeland. To receive such a visa, the foreigner must meet certain requirements that exist under the present U.S. immigration laws.

Our present immigration laws limit the total number of immigrants to about 270,000 a year. Not counted in that total are immediate relatives of U.S. citizens (husbands or wives, and unmarried children under the age of 21); the parents of citizens are also admitted under this rule if the citizens are over the age of 21. (Because of this rule, a person will often come to this country, leaving his or her family behind, and then bring them here after he or she becomes a citizen.) There are a few other special classes of persons who can enter outside the annual total, such as aliens who are or were once employed by the U.S. government.

Of the total number of immigrants allowed in a year, no country can supply more than 20,000. A certain number of places are set aside for particular

Many people try to enter the United States illegally each year. America's border with Mexico is one of the most active entry places for illegal aliens. Shown here are two young Mexicans breaking through a fence along the border.

categories of people. If any of those categories are not filled, the numbers can be allocated to the next category. The first preference is given to the unmarried adult children of U.S. citizens (54,000 places). Next are the spouses (husbands or wives) and unmarried children of legally resident aliens (72,200 plus any places that have been left unfilled from the first-preference category). Third come members of certain professions or those with special skills and abilities in the sciences and the arts (27,000 plus any unfilled places in categories one and two). The fourth category is the married children of U.S. citizens (27,000 plus unused places in categories one to three). Fifth are the brothers and sisters of U.S. citizens who are over age 21

Immigrants eagerly sort through mail carts that contain the results of a visa lottery.

(64,000 plus unused places). Sixth are skilled or unskilled workers for whom there is a special need (27,000 plus). Last of all, if any places in the previous six categories have not been filled, "other qualified applicants" are admitted on a first-come, first-served basis.

Even after a person has qualified for a permanent visa, he or she must often wait for the visa to actually be issued. This might take months.

The Green Card

Permanent resident aliens are given a "green card." This entitles them to work legally in the United States and extends them most of the rights of the U.S. Constitution. Green card holders are required to pay taxes, and males must also register for the Selective Service.

The color of the card was once green. It was changed years ago but the name has stuck.

Refugees

Besides people with temporary and permanent visas, the United States also allows 5,000 refugees a year into the country. These are people who face persecution in their own country because of their political views. They come to the United States seeking political asylum.

After the Vietnam War in the 1970s, thousands of Southeast Asians sought refuge in the United States and other nations. Their homeland lay in

Refugees and illegal aliens line up in Houston to apply for amnesty, which would allow them to stay in the United States legally.

ruins. They opposed Communist rule. These refugees escaped by going to sea in flimsy boats, hoping to be picked up by U.S. or other foreign ships. Many died.

More recently, thousands of Cuban and Haitian refugees have also risked their lives at sea to come here to escape political and economic hardship. In 1980 more than 120,000 Cubans entered the United States after fleeing the Caribbean island nation in what became known as the Mariel boatlift, saying it could not handle and support so many people at one time.

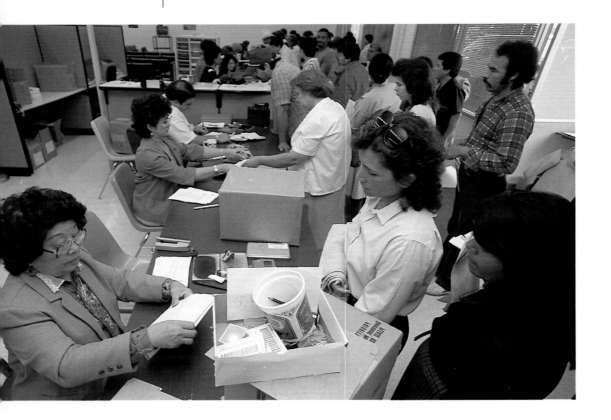

In late 1990, thousands of Haitians fled their island country after a bloody military coup toppled a democratically elected president. In just four months the U.S. Coast Guard picked up more than 16,000 Haitians as they tried to enter the United States. The federal government wanted to return them, arguing that the Haitians left only because they wanted a better life and not for political reasons. The Haitians disagreed. They said that if they were returned they would be killed by the ruling military government. The U.S. Supreme Court ruled that the forced return was legal.

Thousands of Haitian refugees were gathered in holding facilities before they were sent back to Haiti by the U.S. government in 1992.

★ ★ ★ ★ ALEXANDER SOLZHENITSYN: SEEKING ★ ★ ★ ★ POLITICAL ASYLUM IN THE UNITED STATES

Alexander Solzhenitsyn, one of the former Soviet Union's best-known writers, did not come to the United States by choice. The Communist government expelled him in 1974 after the publication of one of his books, and it stripped him of his citizenship.

Solzhenitsyn strongly opposed the human-rights abuses of Soviet governments. He paid a heavy price for his political outspokenness. He was joined by many others.

Born in 1918, Solzhenitsyn first ran afoul of the authorities in 1945 just for writing a letter that criticized the Soviet leader Joseph Stalin. Solzhenitsyn was jailed for eight years.

After serving the prison term and three years of enforced exile, Solzhenitsyn became a math teacher. In his spare time he wrote.

In 1962, at a time when the Soviet authorities had eased some political restrictions, Solzhenitsyn's *One Day in the Life of Ivan Denisovich* was published. The book won immediate acclaim for its powerful description of a typical day in the life of an inmate in one of Stalin's forced-labor camps.

But just two years later Solzhenitsyn was facing mounting criticism from the Soviet authorities. The government-owned publishing company refused to publish any more of Solzhenitsyn's work. Instead he secretly published his books and circulated them among friends. This kind of publishing was known as *samizdat*. His books, such as *The First Circle* (1968) and *The Cancer Ward* (1968), were smuggled out of the Soviet Union and published abroad.

Requirements for Citizenship

The legal process by which a person becomes a U.S. citizen is called "naturalization"; a foreign-born person who becomes a citizen in this way is called a "naturalized citizen." The first requirement for naturalization is that the person has lived in the United States for five years. There are also other requirements: the person must be at least 18 years

In 1970, Solzhenitsyn was awarded the Nobel Prize for Literature, but he declined to go to Stockholm to receive the prestigious award. He feared that if he left, the Soviet authorities would lock him out of his country and not permit him to return.

In late 1973, when the first volume of *The Gulag Archipelago* was published in France, the Soviet press attacked Solzhenitsyn for "slandering" the state. The book describes the cruel prison system that existed under the Communists. (Russians began reading *The Gulag* after the Soviet state began to crumble in the late 1980s.)

Thousands of other people have come to the United States because their political views put them in grave danger if they remained in their homelands. Such individuals came to this nation seeking political asylum.

Alexander Solzhenitsyn

For Solzhenitsyn and many others, the United States was the place they could turn to when they were no longer welcome in their own countries.

old; have a good moral character and be loyal to the United States (green card holders must show that in the five years that they have lived here they have not engaged in any criminal activity or abused drugs or alcohol); be able to understand English; have a knowledge of U.S. history and government; and take the oath of allegiance to the United States.

If a candidate has successfully met all the other requirements and can respond to simple questions regarding the government, the INS, which is in charge of naturalization, recommends that the application for citizenship be granted. The candidate appears before a judge and formally pledges the Oath of Allegiance to the United States. He or she solemnly promises to support and defend the Constitution and the laws of the United States. In return, the new citizen receives a certificate of citizenship as proof that naturalization has been successfully completed. And with it, all the rights, benefits, and responsibilities of U.S. citizenship are granted. For many immigrants, the day they become citizens is the happiest day of their lives.

Today, more than 80 percent of immigrants to the United States come from Latin America and Asia. In 1990, foreign-born persons made up 8.6 percent of all Americans. This rate is expected to climb to 14.2 percent by 2040. Although a rate of 14.2 percent may seem high to some, it is nearly the same as the rate in the late 1800s.

The United States, more than almost any other nation, has relied on immigrants. Each wave of immigration has made its contribution to help build our country. With each wave, the United States has experienced growing pains and concerns that the immigrants would weaken the country. Instead, America has always adjusted and has became healthier and more interesting for it.

Opposite:
Rudolf Nureyev, one of the world's greatest classical dancers, was a political refugee who became a naturalized American citizen.

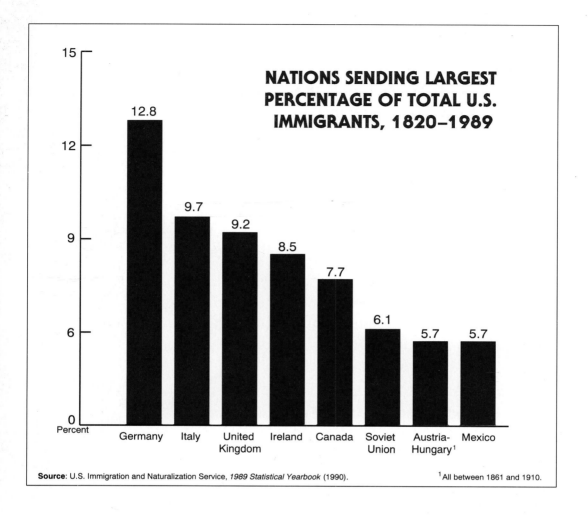

NATIONS SENDING LARGEST PERCENTAGE OF TOTAL U.S. IMMIGRANTS, 1820–1989

	Percent
Germany	12.8
Italy	9.7
United Kingdom	9.2
Ireland	8.5
Canada	7.7
Soviet Union	6.1
Austria-Hungary[1]	5.7
Mexico	5.7

Source: U.S. Immigration and Naturalization Service, *1989 Statistical Yearbook* (1990).

[1] All between 1861 and 1910.

What may pose a greater risk to this nation's health is the public's apathy toward playing an active role as citizens. Less than 50 percent of eligible voters cast ballots at election time, one of the lowest figures in a democratic nation. What's more, many people avoid serving on juries, another responsibility of citizens. The declining sense of civic duty in the United States could damage the partnership between the state and the individual that is at the very heart of citizenship.

Citizenship Day

Americans celebrate their citizenship on September 17. Citizenship Day honors citizens and seeks to remind people that with citizenship come rights and responsibilities. Students in school study the importance of citizenship and often pay tribute to their country by reciting the Pledge of Allegiance.

Although many Americans take their citizenship for granted, those who come here usually don't. Usually they have had to overcome many obstacles. Their decision to become citizens was of their own free will. They know firsthand what makes U.S. citizenship special.

September 17 is set aside to honor our country and its citizens. In observance of Citizenship Day, people across the nation recite the Pledge of Allegiance.

Glossary

abolitionists People who wanted to end slavery before the Civil War.

alien One who was born in another country and does not have citizenship in the country where he or she lives.

apartheid The official separation of people of different races, as in South Africa.

asylum Safety a country offers people who have fled their own countries because of political persecution.

democracy Government by the people, or citizens.

dictatorship Government by one absolute ruler, or dictator.

émigrés People who immigrate because they oppose the politics or governments in their home countries.

immigrant Someone who moves to another country to live permanently.

indentured servant In early U.S. history, a person who was bound to work for an employer, usually for a period of seven years, before being free.

naturalization The process by which an alien becomes a citizen of a country.

refugee A person who flees war, persecution, or some other danger and seeks safety in another country.

visa A document or seal in a passport that grants a foreigner permission to enter a country.

For Further Reading

Ayer, Eleanor. *Our National Monuments.* Brookfield, Connecticut: Millbrook Press, 1992.

Behrens, June. *Miss Liberty: First Lady of the World.* Chicago: Childrens Press, 1986.

Orlov, Ann, and Stolarik, Mark M., eds. *Illegal Aliens.* Broomall, Pennsylvania: Chelsea House, 1991.

Orlov, Ann, and Stolarik, Mark M., eds. *The Immigrant Experience.* Broomall, Pennsylvania: Chelsea House, 1991.

Scher, Linda. *The Vote: Making Your Voice Heard.* Austin, Texas: Raintree Steck-Vaughn, 1993.

Stein, R.C. *Ellis Island.* Chicago: Childrens Press, 1985.

Index